W9-BFD-824

Martin Luther
KING JR.

by Riley Flynn   Consulting Editor: Gail Saunders-Smith, PhD

CAPSTONE PRESS
a capstone imprint

Pebble Books are published by Capstone Press,
1710 Roe Crest Drive, North Mankato, Minnesota 56003
www.capstonepub.com

Library of Congress Cataloging-in-Publication Data
Flynn, Riley.
  Martin Luther King, Jr. / by Riley Flynn.
     pages cm.—(Pebble books. Great African-Americans)
  Summary: "Simple text and photographs present the life of Martin Luther King Jr"—Provided
by publisher.
  Includes bibliographical references and index.
  ISBN 978-1-4765-3953-9 (library binding)
  ISBN 978-1-4765-5157-9 (paperback)
  ISBN 978-1-4765-6014-4 (ebook pdf)
1. King, Martin Luther, Jr., 1929–1968—Juvenile literature. 2. African Americans–
Biography—Juvenile literature. 3. Civil rights workers—United States—Biography—Juvenile
literature. 4. Baptists—United States—Clergy—Biography—Juvenile literature. 5. African
Americans—Civil rights—History—20th century—Juvenile literature. I. Title.
  E185.97.K5F59 2014
  323.092–dc23
  [B]   2013035323

Editorial Credits
Erika L. Shores, editor; Ashlee Suker, designer; Wanda Winch, media researcher;
Laura Manthe, production specialist

Photo Credits
Getty Images: AFP, 8, 18, Mondadori Portfolio, 20, New York Times Co., 4 Time & Life
Pictures/Don Cravens, 14; Library of Congress: Prints and Photographs Division, cover, 12,
16; Newscom: Everett Collection, 10; Shutterstock: kstudija, cover (book design); SuperStock
Inc: Everett Collection, 6

Note to Parents and Teachers

The Great African-Americans set supports national curriculum standards for
social studies related to people, places, and environments. This book describes
and illustrates Martin Luther King Jr. The images support early readers in
understanding the text. The repetition of words and phrases helps early readers
learn new words. This book also introduces early readers to subject-specific
vocabulary words, which are defined in the Glossary section. Early readers may
need assistance to read some words and to use the Table of Contents, Glossary,
Read More, Internet Sites, and Index sections of the book.

Printed in the United States of America in North Mankato, Minnesota.
092013   007764CGS14

Table of Contents

4

Meet Martin

Martin Luther King Jr. was a minister and peacemaker. He fought for freedom and equality for everyone. Martin was a leader of the American Civil Rights Movement.

Martin (front, right) and his family

1929

born

6

Young Martin

Martin was born in Georgia in 1929.
His father was a minister. The elementary
school that Martin went to was only
for African-Americans. Martin lived
in a place with segregation laws. These
laws kept blacks and whites separate.

Coretta and Martin in 1956

1929

born

1953

marries
Coretta Scott

Martin was smart. His teachers let him skip grades 9 and 12. In college Martin decided to become a minister. After college Martin went to Massachusetts. He met Coretta Scott. They married in 1953.

Martin speaks to reporters in 1956

1929	1953	1954	1955
born	marries Coretta Scott	moves to Alabama	earns doctorate

As an Adult

In 1954 Martin and Coretta moved to Alabama. Martin became Dr. King in 1955 after earning his doctorate. Later that year Martin was inspired by an African-American woman named Rosa Parks.

1929	1953	1954	1955
born	marries Coretta Scott	moves to Alabama	earns doctorate

Rosa Parks was riding a bus in Montgomery, Alabama, one day in 1955. She was told to give her seat to a white person. She said no. Rosa was arrested. The arrest led to the Montgomery bus boycott.

African-Americans refused to ride Montgomery city buses.

1929	**1953**	**1954**	**1955**
born	marries Coretta Scott	moves to Alabama	earns doctorate

Martin helped lead the protest against bus segregation laws. For 381 days African-Americans stopped riding Montgomery buses. In 1956 the Supreme Court ruled bus segregation was illegal. After the boycott Martin and his family moved to Atlanta.

| **1929** | **1953** | **1954** | **1955** |
| born | marries Coretta Scott | moves to Alabama | earns doctorate |

16

Later Years

Martin was an excellent public speaker. One of his greatest speeches was given in Washington, D.C., in 1963. Martin gave his "I Have a Dream" speech during a march in support of a civil rights bill.

1963

gives "I Have a Dream" speech

1929	1953	1954	1955
born	marries Coretta Scott	moves to Alabama	earns doctorate

18

Congress passed the Civil Rights Act in 1964. This bill ended segregation in public places. That same year Martin was given the Nobel Prize for Peace. Martin had done the most toward gaining world peace that year.

1963
gives "I Have a Dream" speech

1964
wins Nobel Prize

People filled the streets for Martin's funeral on April 9, 1968.

1929
born

1953
marries
Coretta Scott

1954
moves to
Alabama

1955
earns doctorate

Martin was killed in 1968. He wanted

all people to be free and equal.

Martin believed in peace and fairness.

People remember him for his beliefs.

On Martin Luther King Jr. Day

in January we celebrate his life

and work.

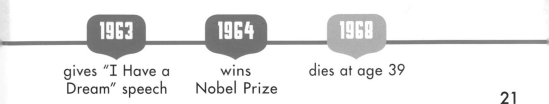

1963
gives "I Have a
Dream" speech

1964
wins
Nobel Prize

1968
dies at age 39

Glossary

arrest—to stop and hold someone for doing something against the law

bill—a written idea for a new law

boycott—to refuse to take part in something as a way of showing support for an idea or group of people

civil rights—the rights that all people have to freedom and equality under the law

Congress—the part of the U.S. government that makes laws

doctorate—the highest degree a person can earn from a college or university

equality—being equal

inspire—to influence or encourage other people in a good way

minister—a person who leads a church

segregation—separating people because of their skin color

Read More

Gosman, Gillian. *Martin Luther King Jr.* Life Stories. New York: PowerKids Press, 2011.

Hall, M.C. *Martin Luther King, Jr. Day.* Little World Holidays and Celebrations. Vero Beach, Fla.: Rourke Pub., 2011.

Nelson, Maria. *Coretta Scott King.* Civil Rights Crusaders. New York: Gareth Stevens Pub., 2012.

Internet Sites

FactHound offers a safe, fun way to find Internet sites related to this book. All of the sites on FactHound have been researched by our staff.

Here's all you do:
Visit *www.facthound.com*
Type in this code: 9781476539539

Check out projects, games and lots more at
www.capstonekids.com

Critical Thinking Using the Common Core

1. Segregation means to keep people apart because of their skin color. What are two kinds of segregation discussed in this book? (Key Ideas and Details)

2. The Civil Rights Act ended legal segregation. Some people think African-Americans and white people still aren't treated equally. What do you think? Use Internet and print sources to support your ideas. (Integration of Knowledge and Ideas)

Index

Word Count: 318
Grade: 1
Early-Intervention Level: 24